TOTALLY NAKED ©

A Guide to Living Life Inside Out

Ebonie M. Ware, MSW, CSW

ISBN 978-0692896808

Printed in the United Stated of America

This book is dedicated to the loving memory of my mother and the novel she never had the chance to complete. As long as I am living, I will strive to be the author you always dreamt of being.

Table of Contents

Introduction

There is a calling on your life that is waiting to be fulfilled. There is no mistake that you have selected this book. If you are like me, you do not believe in coincidences. You believe that God puts us in the right place at the right time. This life can be difficult to navigate. We have "stuff," that gets in the way of our destiny. Whether it is our relationships, careers, or past experiences, our lives can become complicated.

In the midst of all of our "stuff," we often lose sight of our potential. Trust me it is there, we just have to be intentional in our search for it. The purpose of this motivational guide is to help you to look beyond the surface of your life. Totally Naked is described as stripping down to your purest form while learning to see yourself the way God sees you.

I am a witness to the power of faith and persistence no matter the circumstance. I know how it feels to live a life of fear and confusion. It is up to us to make the decision to look past our understanding and learn to trust what God has already approved. I created this motivational guide to help you experience living in truth. With an educational background in Social Work, I am fully aware of the many challenges that stand in the way of our purpose. The good news is we can break through. With a little faith and action, anything is possible. I am honored that you have chosen this book to assist with your upcoming journey. Remember the truth is better naked.

A Servant's Prayer

Dear Lord, give me the courage and the wisdom to overcome the fear that constantly delays my journey. Let me not be concerned with the things that I do not know or do not have, but stay fixated on my potential. I still have that spirit inside of me that will not let me rest until it is done. Now what that is, I am not sure. But dear God I will not stop until I know. I need your strength more than ever now. I pray that these words will float in the universe and ride the wings of angels.

Please don't let me stand in my own way. I am excited about sharing my beauty with this world. I am elated about carrying out your purpose. I ask to be kept in your care and cradled in your love. I know it is up to me to stay because I know that you will never let me go. Let the negative and hurtful words of my enemies roll away like the tides of the ocean. Who shall I fear when I know who holds my future?

From the beginning, to the deepest corner of my soul, I ask thee to give me strength to finish this race; with open arms and a clean heart. I am determined because I believe in all that you have for me. I voice this prayer with total humility and faith in your power. Amen.

If you are constantly wondering why you just can't seem to get settled, it's probably because you are not where you need to be.

Confirmation

If you are reading this, it is probably because you are ready for a change. This life is complicated. If we are not careful, we can be swallowed up by a sea of uncertainty. It is easier to travel the path covered in footprints. We learn to walk aimlessly in the same direction because we are afraid to test out unfamiliar territory. We become numb to mediocrity and learn to suppress our need for something greater.

We all have our own journeys to navigate. Our life events are tailor made to mold us into the individuals we are meant to be. Of course we will make mistakes along the way. There will be unexpected circumstances to distract us from our path. Some of us answer quickly to the voice inside, while others may need something louder and more colorful to awaken them.

Don't be discouraged by your setbacks and disappointments. These obstacles only make your story more interesting. You become more relatable and someone will gain the momentum they need just by knowing you are not super human. You were just blessed with an extraordinary gift and decided to use it. We all have a choice. We can run from our destiny or choose to embrace it.

Our inner power haunts some of us. It won't allow us to settle for the norm. We are plagued by the idea of a purposeful life. It is no mistake that you have chosen this book. You are at the end of something and ready to start a new journey. There is something inside that won't let you accept the life you are currently living.

You will never truly be happy unless you answer whatever it is that is calling. If you are still reading, this book is for you. Don't be afraid to live from the inside out. In order to discover your authentic self, you must be willing to strip away those things that are holding you back. You must be willing to live in your purest form. The truth is better naked.

Imagine the places you could go if you would just let go.

Totally Naked

Who are you? Would you be able to answer this question without hesitation? We spend a lot of time masking who we really are. We have stuff, stuff that distracts us from having to think about what we really want. Our lives become complicated. We get tangled in obligations that keep us from going beyond the surface. We don't have time to dig deep. We have jobs. We have kids. We have relationships that occupy our existence. We have roles to play.

Now, these roles certainly enrich our lives and help mold our character. They are extremely important in shaping who we are. But, it is often those very things we live for that cause us to lose our way. It is much easier to focus on the needs of others than to deal with your desires. So what is it that you want or need? Are you happy with the life you are currently living? Have you even had time to think about it?

We all have gifts. Gifts that make our lives more fulfilling. You may already be aware of your gift or talent. Some of us know what makes us happy but need a little push getting there. Others have no idea what drives them to reach their full potential. Then there are those that are somewhere in the middle. Wherever you may be, looking at your life from the inside out can be beneficial.

Totally Naked means stripping down to your purest form, while learning to see yourself the way God sees you. We have layers. It is so human of us to complicate our lives. It is much easier to cover up our potential. If we focus on everything but our purpose, we avoid the risk of failure. We avoid the what-ifs in life. Let's face it; the what-ifs can be scary. The idea of putting your best foot forward and receiving nothing in return can be down-right terrifying.

What if I told you that you are not alone? The good news is God is waiting for you to step out on faith. We often make the mistake of thinking we have to have it all figured out. Guess what, God just wants to know that you believe in what is waiting for you. You will soon realize that once you take that leap, the right people, places, and things, will start gravitating toward you. This is not a coincidence. This is your faith and actions coming back full circle. The power of prayer and action is incredible!

Learning to be totally naked is a process. We all have things in our lives that challenge our truth. We must learn to remove those things, or at least push them aside until we discover our purpose. Once we can see ourselves for who we really are, it makes it easier to make moves in the right direction. No, this won't happen overnight, and no one said it would be easy. It takes practice. We have to exercise our minds and get in the habit of thinking effectively.

The purpose of the Totally Naked Motivational Guide is to get you in the habit of thinking critically. Each exercise was uniquely designed to assist readers in developing a better understanding of their purpose. It is important to be completely honest. The good news is this was designed for your personal growth. There is no overseer or right or wrong answer. This is simply a guide created to assist you with getting your life on the right track. There is no answer key or scale to measure your responses. No answer will be identical. These activities are carefully constructed to help the reader dig deep on a personal level.

The concept of being totally naked is based on the idea that when we strip down to our true selves, it is easier to find our purpose. We have a better understanding of what God is saying when we get rid of some of the noise. We learn to get down to the basics, and start looking at the bigger picture. Our day to day lives makes it difficult to think critically about what we really want or need in life. It is always a good idea to take the time to deeply consider what we were put on this earth to accomplish.

Before you begin, I would suggest finding a quiet place to work. Try to find time in your hectic schedule designated solely to this book. You will find space for your responses after the introduction of each activity. Please use a pencil for these exercises. You want to use pencils because you will find yourself editing your responses. There is no specific time that it should be completed. Go at your own pace. This guide was not designed to be completed in one sitting. It requires deep concentration. It requires you to go beyond the surface of your life. You may have to travel to an unwanted territory.

There may be circumstances in your life that you have tried hard to forget. Although they are painful to revisit, these events could be essential to your personal growth. There are people, places, and things that play a major part in our current situations. Sometimes we are affected by events we haven't thought about in years. We are like emotional zombies wandering the earth. We go numb to our feelings of pain and discontentment.

We learn to accept the lives we are living. We go with the flow and grow accustomed to existing in a way that doesn't serve us or others. Simply existing; not living. If you are reading this book, I believe that you want more. You are curious about a life of happiness and purpose. You are ready to make a change. Take a deep breath and let's get started!

Face Value

The face value section was designed as an introduction. Simply answer these basic questions about yourself. Your birthplace, names of immediate family members, religious affiliation, etc. As simple as this seems, these are questions most of us have not thought about in awhile. This basic information helps to jumpstart you into thinking critically. This helps to grease your engine. You have a long journey ahead. You want to make sure you are well equipped.

The second portion of the face value section asks for you to think about some of your greatest attributes as well as your weaknesses. Take a moment and reflect on what makes you great. Yes, great! Don't underestimate your contributions to the world. What do you feel that you contribute to your family and friends? Maybe you are a part of a group or organization. What do you add to your job or career? It can be difficult to reflect on our qualities, but it is essential to our growth. How will you know where you need to go if you don't know where you are?

What about your shortcomings? Think about some areas that you need to work on. We all have things that make us feel less confident. Brainstorm about parts of your life that you would like to improve. Being aware of our weaknesses gives us the opportunity to focus on areas of need. It is ok to not be great at everything. We are human. Our imperfections make us unique.

The only way to better understand our strengths and weaknesses is to study them. We have to be fully aware of our contributions as well as areas we fall short. Just because we are not good at something doesn't mean we cannot practice. A little faith and practice will go a long way. Don't rush through this section. It is important to be cognizant of the ugly and the beautiful. Sometimes our vulnerability brings out the best in us. So don't be afraid to let go!

Face Value: Who are you?

Name _____

Children_____

D.O.B. _____

Where were you born? _____

Mother: _____

Father: _____

Siblings: _____

Religious Affiliation_____

Education_____ (Highest level)

(5 of your greatest Attributes)   **(5 Areas needing change)**

1._____   1._____

2._____   2_____

3._____   3._____

4._____   4._____

5._____   5._____

Face Value: Who Are You?

_____

_____

_____

_____

_____

_____

_____

_____

_____

_____

_____

_____

_____

_____

_____

_____

_____

_____

Face Value

_____

_____

_____

_____

_____

_____

_____

_____

_____

_____

_____

_____

_____

_____

_____

_____

_____

Face Value

Face Value

Face Value

The In-between

There is a unique time in-between birth and death called life. How we choose to spend it is up to us. Yes, there will be circumstances that are out of our control. We experience some rough patches along the way; some more painful than others. We can choose how to react and deal with what we experience. We also have to keep in mind that life doesn't just happen to us, we happen to life. The decisions we make can directly affect our paths.

It is important to think about what mark you wish to leave on this earth. What type of impact to do you want to have on the lives of your children? How will you affect the lives of others? What do you want to experience in this lifetime? Is your life on the right course to make this happen? Maybe you are not sure what you really want. This exercise may be uncomfortable for some. It can appear a little morbid but trust me it is important. In this section you will find a sample obituary. Take time to read it slowly. Pay attention to the subjects mentioned. You will find a person who lived a life of love, accomplishment, and service. Does this ignite anything in you?

Think about your life. Do you feel that you are living a fulfilling life? Do you feel that you are on the right path? This section may be somewhat difficult to complete. No one wants to think about leaving this earth. Although it is an undesirable topic, it is something that we must all experience. No one is exempt. We all have an expiration date. Unfortunately, we have no idea just how much time we have. This is why it is so important to be intentional with how we spend our time.

Take a moment to complete the blank obituary form. Spend time brainstorming about how you would want your obituary to read. The purpose of this exercise is not to focus on death but to really think about life. Thinking about the things you want to happen before you leave this earth will help guide you to the right path. We have to be aware of the steps it will take to accomplish these events.

What do you wish to achieve? Are you spending your time with the right people? Are you going to the right places? We began to realize that life is more strategic than we think when we learn to take control. Although we do not have total power over what happens to us, we can steer the ship in the right direction. Utilize this section to assist you with thinking about what is most important. Your obituary should give a true snapshot of the life you wish to live. Be honest and take your time.

Sample Obituary

Jane Smith died yesterday at the age of 89 from complications related to surgery. Mrs. Smith is preceded in death by her husband, David Smith. She is survived by two children: Laura Brown and George Smith; three grandchildren and four great-grandchildren. From a young age, Mrs. Smith was always an active and energetic person who loved being outdoors. While still in high school, she was a part of a dance team, the school newspaper, and the debate team. She even created her own social club with her peers.

Mrs. Jane Smith and her husband founded the Share a Life Foundation which gives necessary resources to children in need in their community. This organization, for the past 50 years, has provided food, school supplies, and tutoring services to school-aged children. The Smith family worked diligently year after year to make this organization a continued success.

Since her husband's death ten years ago, Mrs. Smith was active in creating community projects to help children be more active and successful in their environments. The Share a Life Foundation has assisted hundreds of at-risk children with graduating from high school and enrolling into credible universities. Mrs. Smith also spearheaded projects to create afterschool programs for children needing socialization and leadership skills. In the last years of her life, she slowed down a bit as hip trouble limited her mobility and a string of illnesses found her in hospitalized care. Her children and grandchildren remained by her side through it all.

Services will be held at Millard Funeral home June 22nd at 1:00 pm; Followed by burial at Wilmington cemetery.

Complete your Obituary on the following page.

The In-Between: Obituary

Obituary

_____

_____

_____

_____

_____

_____

_____

_____

_____

_____

_____

_____

_____

_____

_____

_____

_____

_____

Obituary

_____

_____

_____

_____

_____

_____

_____

_____

_____

_____

_____

_____

_____

_____

_____

_____

_____

_____

_____

Obituary

_____

_____

_____

_____

_____

_____

_____

_____

_____

_____

_____

_____

_____

_____

_____

_____

_____

Obituary

_____

_____

_____

_____

_____

_____

_____

_____

_____

_____

_____

_____

_____

_____

_____

_____

_____

_____

_____

Obituary

No one will remember that you had to start over; they will remember how you finished.

General Self-Analysis (GSA)

The next section is the General Self-Analysis. The purpose of this portion is to get a better idea of where you are currently. Do you compare your life to the lives of others? If so, how do you view your life in comparison to others? Do you feel that you are where you want to be in life? Do you consider yourself a happy person? These questions may be difficult to answer. It is possible that you have never taken deep consideration into where you are in life.

It is essential to be aware of the position you are in. The only way to make positive change is to be knowledgeable of what needs changing. When maintaining a garden, a gardener must treat the roots in order for the plants to grow. We have to go beneath the surface if we want to make real progress. Dealing with the surface of your life is not sustainable and will leave you in a constant state of confusion. There is more to you than what meets the eye.

Take a moment to answer these questions. Be honest about how you see yourself. Remember no one is watching but you. You are the only one with access to these records. It may seem repetitive to ask for honesty continuously, but trust me it is necessary. It is human nature for us to want things to appear better than what they are, even with ourselves.

Allow yourself to let go. Remember that this is for your personal growth. There is no way to move forward without acknowledging the desire to leave your current position. Don't be embarrassed by where you are, especially when you know that you want more. There is beauty in knowing that things can be better and that we have the power to change.

General Self-Analysis (GSA)

1. Do you often compare your life to the lives of others? If so, how do you view your life in comparison to others?

2. Do you feel that you are doing everything you can to live the life you want to live?

3. If you could change one thing about your current situation what would that be?

4. Do you feel that you are where you want to be in life?

5. Do you consider yourself a happy person?

Complete GSA on the following page.

General Self-Analysis

General Self Analysis

General Self-Analysis

General Self Analysis

General Self-Analysis

Don't be discouraged... Be determined to change what is discouraging you.

Motivation

Psychologist Abraham Maslow proposed the following exercise in 1943. Yes I know 1943 was a long time ago, but trust me this model is still relevant today. Maslow constructed a five tier model of human needs. Maslow (1943, 1954) stated that people are motivated to achieve certain needs and that some take precedent over others (Mcleod 2007). The first four stages deal with deficits in our lives. The idea is that we are motivated to make a change when certain needs are not being met.

These needs starting with the most basic are listed as Biological/Psychological, Safety, Social, and Esteem. Our biological needs cover our basic survival needs such as water, food, shelter, and health. When we lack in one of these areas we often find ways to meet our needs. For example, if you are unable to provide food on your table for yourself or your children, you may be motivated to find a second job or pick up more shifts at work.

If you are feeling unsafe in a bad relationship, you may be motivated to seek help from authorities or contact other support systems. The point of the matter is, when we lack in an area we will find the means to satisfy that need. Some situations may take longer than others, especially as you get to the more abstract stages.

Self-actualization is the last stage. This stage discusses a human beings need to reach their full potential. At this level, an individual is searching for purpose; the need to express a gift or talent is realized. We may recognize our gifts during other stages, but it is in the self-actualization stage that a person begins to focus on whatever they wish to do or become. Obtaining this level of clarity in our lives can be difficult, but not impossible. It takes belief in oneself, hard work, and concentration. We have to be intentional in our decision-making process.

Maslow's Hierarchy of Needs

What is your Motivation?

Levels of Need:

***Biological and Physiological Needs**- basic survival needs such as food, water, shelter, health, etc.

***Safety Needs**-Freedom from war/ conflict. A need for protection/ stability.

***Social Needs**- Love, family, affection, work group, support system, etc.

***Esteem Needs**- Independence, responsibility, status, prestige, achievement, etc.

***Self-actualization needs**- Personal growth and fulfillment; PURPOSE.

Now that you are more familiar with Maslow's motivational model, take a moment to apply it to your life. Complete the Maslow's self-analysis exercise. Go through each stage and list the things in your life that you may be lacking. Start with the basics and finish with the more complex areas. For example, if you have a desire to ask for a promotion at work but lack the confidence to do so, you would list it under the esteem needs. Maybe, you continue to accept bad relationships. This would fall under social needs; the need to belong or feel loved.

Remember to take your time. There is no rush. You want to make sure to focus on each aspect of your life. Think about the areas that need improvement. Think about where you may fall short. This exercise is essential because it gives you a better grasp of where you are. Don't cheat yourself by being dishonest about your life.

You are the only one who knows where you stand. If you choose not to start from the beginning, it will be almost impossible to get to the finish line. Keep in mind that this is all for your personal development. Spend ample time on each level of need. You will begin to establish a foundation to build on.

Self-Analysis of Maslow's Hierarchy

List your needs in the following Areas…

**Biological and
Physiological**

Safety Needs

Social Needs

Esteem Needs

**Self-
Actualization**

Motivation: Maslow's Hierarchy of Needs

_____

_____

_____

_____

_____

_____

_____

_____

_____

_____

_____

_____

_____

_____

_____

_____

_____

Motivation

Motivation

Motivation

Motivation

_____

_____

_____

_____

_____

_____

_____

_____

_____

_____

_____

_____

_____

_____

_____

_____

_____

In order to have peace in your life,
you must have a piece of mind.

Reflection

There are comforting places we often travel to in our minds. Reminiscing on good times spent with loved ones and friends; a beautiful vacation; affection from our children. These places are easy to locate because they bring a sense of happiness and peace. When there is trouble in our current situations, good memories can help to ease the pain. They help us to remember a time when things were better; a time when our lives felt good. We cherish these moments and file them away in a safe place.

Although it is important to keep up with the "feel good" memories, there are others that can be just as important to our growth. You know the forgotten ones. The ones we bury so deep in the sand that the tide can't wash them up; the ones that show up uninvited and disguise themselves. We feel hurt and anger but have no idea why.

These emotions stem from hurtful places that we refuse to revisit. Some, we never acknowledged as an issue. These people, places, and things, are like ghost haunting our future and hindering our progression. As the saying goes "We cannot fix what we don't acknowledge." We have to be willing to go deeper than the surface. Our best potential can be found deep within us.

This exercise was intentionally constructed for deep sea fishing. You may have to go down in the pit of your memory banks. Remember, this is intended to be difficult. There is no right or wrong answer or an easy way out. The purpose of this activity is to help you get a better understanding of what is affecting you. Good or bad.

When we are aware of what triggers our emotions, we are more equipped to deal with it and move forward. In this portion of the book you are asked to reflect on three of the most significant events in your life. It could be the death of a loved one, heartbreak, birth of a child, or a career change. Some of these events may not be pleasant to think about, but may play a major role in your development.

Again, make sure you are in a quiet place. Try your best to eliminate any distractions. This is your time to examine your life. You want to dissect each significant moment as much as possible.

When we learn to pin point the things that most affect us, we can learn to react to them in an appropriate manner. So buckle your seat belt and get ready for takeoff. It's time to travel back in time.

Reflection Selection

Reflect on 3 of the most significant events in your life. Some of these events may not be pleasant to think about, but may play a major role in who you are. Our experiences often explain some of the decisions we make and our current lifestyle. Take time to think deeply about the events that have most impacted your life.

1.

2.

3.

Complete Reflection activity on the following page.

Reflection

Reflection

Reflection

Reflection

Reflection

Push harder than you knew you could…Go places you never thought you would.

Systems

We are very complex beings. It is difficult to sum up our lives in a few words or statements. There are so many layers protecting our core that we often lose sight of our center. Systems theory has been used as a guide for social work practice. The theory explains that an effective system is based on individual needs, rewards, expectations, and attributes of the people living in the system (Simmons, 2014.) Our lives can be complicated. The more we learn to simplify our lives, the more we can focus on what is most important.

So what is most important? Have you thought about the things in your life that mean the most? Do you feel that the life you are living is a reflection of those things? At times, the lives we live do not coordinate with what we voice as important. This can leave us in a state of confusion. There is no focus and no motivation. We can slip into a life of monotony. We settle for anything and stand for nothing. We learn to live a life that is not our own. If you feel this way, it is not too late to change the course of your life. You just have to be aware of what needs changing.

Take a moment and think about your life. Who do you surround yourself with? Where do you spend most of your time? Where is your focus? In this next section, choose the 5 areas of your life which are most important. Think about if these areas match the life you are currently living. Are you happy with the areas that you have chosen? Think about ways that these aspects of life could improve. The next step in this exercise requests for you to write a sentence about how you would like these areas to be in your life. For example, if you choose religion, you may write a sentence like… "I want a closer relationship with God."

Once you have written down a goal, it makes it easier to focus. Now you see what it is that you would like to accomplish. This helps simplify the process. The next step would be working on how to make this possible. If you wish to have a closer relationship with God, there are certain things you may want to consider; Such as, studying your bible, attending church services, or finding a religious group. Remember, it is not our responsibility to have it all figured out, we just need to make steps in the right direction.

Choose the 5 areas of life which are most important. Number them according to their level of importance. (#1 being most important)

Family _____ Education_____ Career_____

Finance _____Religion/Spirituality _____Friendship_____

Community_____ Health_____ Social_____

Think about the areas of life that you have chosen as most important. Do they reflect the life that you are currently living? Does your current path match the areas of life you value the most? Are you happy with the condition of these areas you have chosen?

Write one sentence about how you would like these areas to be in your life. **Ex: I would like to have a closer relationship with God.**

1.

2.

3.

4.

5.

Systems

Systems

_____

_____

_____

_____

_____

_____

_____

_____

_____

_____

_____

_____

_____

_____

_____

_____

_____

_____

_____

Systems

Systems

_____

_____

_____

_____

_____

_____

_____

_____

_____

_____

_____

_____

_____

_____

_____

Systems

Who but you can live your life and your dreams? You were built for this; live like you own it!

Creatures of Habit

We are fairly predictable. Even those who are most adventurous have common themes which interest them. Although our lives are very complex, we simplify them with certain habits. It is essential to pay attention to these predictable behaviors because they are a reflection of who we are.

In this final exercise you should begin piecing some things together. Think about what makes you happy. Picture yourself wherever brings you most joy. What are you doing? Are you singing? Are you crafting or writing poetry? Maybe you are traveling or volunteering. Next, think about what you do well? What do others usually notice or say about you?

Think about how often you find yourself doing the things you find the most joy. Brainstorm about the things you do well in different areas of your life. For example, maybe you enjoy singing and you find yourself singing in your church choir, and singing in local community events. You find happiness in singing and it shows up in various parts of your life. Once you have pinpointed these activities your mental light bulb should get brighter.

When you discover the same attribute being utilized in different areas of your life, you may have found your gift! You know it is a gift when it comes naturally. It is almost effortless. Others may be amazed by it, but it is often difficult for you to realize just how special it really is.

Once you begin to own your craft you will see the beauty unfold. People, places, and things will be drawn to you. Opportunities you could have never imagined will seem to appear out of the sky. So deeply think about what you find yourself doing often in various areas of your life. It may take some time to recognize the patterns you have created, but they are there.

Use these key areas listed on the Creatures of Habit exercise to write down the similarities of interests in different aspects of your life. You may have never thought about how often you use the same talents or gifts in these different areas. This tells you, no matter the pattern, they are significant.

This should bring you closer to locating your purpose. Trust me it is there. It has been there all along. You just have to be strategic in your search for it. It requires deep consideration and practice. It takes focus and dedication. This is not easy to achieve but it is definitely worth it!

Patterns of Interest

- ❖ **Family/Relationships**
- ❖ **Career/Jobs**
- ❖ **Social/Recreation**

There are many aspects of life we participate in regularly. Do you recognize any common interests in these areas? When you look back over the years, you may find patterns of interest in different parts of your life. For example:

Social:

-I have enjoyed being in a group setting with women; helping them talk through relationships/ issues.

-I enjoy writing pieces to encourage self-love and empowerment geared towards women.

- I enjoy reading books regarding women empowerment.

Career: - I studied Social Work with an interest in women/community.

-I worked for a company geared towards improving women's mental wellness.

Family: I enjoy counseling my family with issues facing them; particularly women.

Common Interest: Empowering women.

Patterns of Interest

1.

2.

3.

4

5.

Complete POI activity on the following page.

Creatures of Habit: Patterns of Interest

_____

_____

_____

_____

_____

_____

_____

_____

_____

_____

_____

_____

_____

_____

_____

_____

_____

Creatures of Habit

Creatures of Habit

_____

_____

_____

_____

_____

_____

_____

_____

_____

_____

_____

_____

_____

_____

_____

_____

_____

Creatures of Habit

_____

_____

_____

_____

_____

_____

_____

_____

_____

_____

_____

_____

_____

_____

_____

_____

_____

_____

Creatures of Habit

_____

_____

_____

_____

_____

_____

_____

_____

_____

_____

_____

_____

_____

_____

_____

_____

_____

_____

Closing

If you are reading this, congratulations, you have completed your workbook! It is important that you are completely honest with each portion of this book. These activities are intended to assist you with developing a better understanding of your purpose. If used appropriately, it can be a foundation for your upcoming journey. Don't be afraid to let go and remove your layers. Once you begin to peel back the fear, doubt, pain, and disappointment, you will find a strength you never knew you had. You will begin to see yourself the way God sees you. You will learn to live in your purest form and walk in purpose.

This may sound unattainable. You may think that others have something that you don't. You may think it is for some and not for others. I have good news for you… it is for whoever chooses to listen. It is for those who make the decision to answer what is calling them. A major difference between those who do and those who don't is persistence.

You have to be intentional. You have to be focused. You have to open your mind and heart to the possibility of living a better life. The life you are meant to live. Will there still be fear, pain, and disappointment? Absolutely! We are not exempt from feeling these emotions. But, when you walk in your purpose, your reaction to these feelings will change. You will learn to deal with unwanted experiences in a more positive manner. It will be easier to bounce back because you know that your future is bright. You know that God is in control of your destiny!

It is much easier to expect failure and live a life of low expectations. If we don't ask or require much, we can avoid disappointment. Many of us fear those thoughts that we can't control. There is something in us that yearns for greatness, but we often shy away from it. What is it that makes us feel like we don't deserve the best? Take a moment, wherever you are and tell yourself "It is ok to receive good things." This may seem silly, but believe me it works.

We have to become accustomed to expecting great things in our lives. Why would we believe that someone else deserves good things but we do not? Once you allow yourself to expect goodness, you will no longer concern yourself with what others have. You can learn to be happy for others and be inspired by their journeys. You will stop and think; if they can, I can too. So ask yourself what do you want for your life? What steps can you take to get there? If you know that God has blessed you with good things, own them. Don't run away from your purpose. God expects greatness and we should too. Do not be afraid to live in your truth!

Now that you have completed your workbook, you have made progress towards your purpose. You should be excited that you have invested in your future. This workbook should not be looked at once and tucked away. Treat it more like a study guide. The more you utilize it the more prepared you will be for the test. You will begin to learn more about yourself and what is important to you.

We all know the saying "Practice makes perfect." Keep this in a place that you visit often.

Make sure it is visible so that it becomes a daily reminder. Set aside time in your busy schedule to go over your responses. You may need to make some adjustments. There may be things that you missed the first or second time around. Be patient and thorough. If used appropriately there is a great chance that this could be life changing! So give yourself permission to go beyond the surface and dig deep into your emotions. Remember the truth is better naked. Good luck on your upcoming journey!

Totally Naked Quotes

1. Until you are honest with yourself, it doesn't matter who is telling you the truth.

2. When you walk in purpose, God is intentional and your efforts won't go in vain; Trust the process.

3. Life does not just happen to us…We have the power to have more desirable experiences.

4. Once you get the right gust of wind beneath your wings, it will be hard to land. You were born to fly!

5. Life is tough, but we were born tougher. Don't fold when faced with adversity. You were not made to fail.

6. Do not envy those who laugh and dance freely…Find your own wings so that you too can rise above conformity.

7. Live your dreams with your eyes wide open.

Additional Notes

Additional Notes

References

Simons Staff. (2014).Theories used in social work practice and practice models , *1*. Retrieved from https://socialwork.simmons.edu/theories-used-social-work-practice

Mcleod, S. (2007) Maslow's Hierarchy of need, 1. Retrieved from https://simplypsychology.org/maslow.html

www.ingramcontent.com/pod-product-compliance
Lightning Source LLC
Chambersburg PA
CBHW052159090426
42741CB00010B/2339